B. B. King

by Eryn Kline Rosenbaum

HOUGHTON MIFFLIN HARCOURT
School Publishers

PHOTOGRAPHY CREDITS: **Cover** © Fabrice Coffrini/epa/CORBIS. **Title page** © Michael Ochs Archives/CORBIS. **2** © Fabrice Coffrini/epa/CORBIS. **4** © Bettmann/CORBIS. **5** © Walter Sanders/Time & Life Pictures/Getty Images. **8** © Michael Ochs Archives/CORBIS. **10** (l) © Hulton Archive/Getty Images. (r) © Agence France Presse/Getty Images. **11** © Paulo Whitaker/Reuters/CORBIS. **12** © Chris Graythen/Getty Images. **14** © Michael Ochs Archives/Getty Images. **18** © Steve Crise/CORBIS.

Printed in China

ISBN-13: 978-0-547-01772-3
ISBN-10: 0-547-01772-3

4 5 6 7 8 0940 18 17 16 15 14 13 12 11 10

B. B. King began singing when he was four years old. When he was eighty-one, he received a Presidential Medal of Freedom for his long career as a great musician. B. B. King sang the blues, and he sang them well.

What are the blues? Feeling sad is sometimes called feeling blue. In the early history of the United States, most African Americans lived in slavery. They developed a style of singing and playing that helped them express their deepest emotions. They called it "the blues," and they made it into a distinctively American, soulful style of music. During his long and brilliant career, B. B. King brought this music to people all over the world. He became a legend: The King of the Blues.

B. B. King is one of the greatest blues musicians in the world.

Growing Up in Mississippi

The man who became B. B. King was born Riley B. King, near Indianola, Mississippi, in 1925. Young Riley had a hard childhood. When he was about four, his parents separated. Riley lived mostly with his grandmother on large cotton farms called plantations. He worked the fields with the adults, plowing, planting, and picking cotton. He had two favorite activities. The first was going to school, when he could get away from working. The second was listening to music and singing in church.

When Riley was nine, his mother died. A few years later, his grandmother died, too. Riley stayed in the little house that he and his grandmother had shared. He made his own living, as if he were an adult.

When Riley's father learned that his son was living alone, he brought Riley to live with him. Riley came to love his father's family, but he was homesick. He returned to Kilmichael, where he had lived with his grandmother, after just a few months. Later, he moved closer to Indianola.

Making Music

Since the time he was a small boy, Riley had been fascinated by music. He loved listening to people singing—"shouting" the blues, as they called it —while they worked in the fields. He loved visiting his Aunt Mima, who owned a phonograph player and about fifty records. He also loved the gospel music of his church.

After church on Sundays, the pastor of his church, Reverend Archie Fair, sometimes ate dinner with Riley and his relatives. Reverend Fair would bring his guitar and leave it on a bed in another room during dinner.

In the early part of the 1900s, many African American people worked as sharecroppers. Sharecroppers worked on land that belonged to a farmer in exchange for a place to live and a portion of the crops.

Beale Street in Memphis, Tennessee, in the 1950s

When the reverend wasn't looking, Riley would pick up the guitar and try to play it. One day, the reverend caught him. Reverend Fair immediately recognized Riley's passion for music and taught him three simple chords, or groups of notes. These chords formed the basis of many of the songs that B. B. King would later write.

Like a Kid in a Candy Store

Riley bought his first guitar when he was about fifteen. He practiced as much as he could when he wasn't working, and played for dimes on the street corners of Indianola. He joined a small group called "The Famous St. John Gospel Singers," but they weren't famous at all. Riley tried to talk them into moving to Memphis, Tennessee, where there were more opportunities for musicians.

In the 1940s, Memphis was one place where they might have a shot at fame. But the other members of the group didn't want to leave Indianola.

Riley got married and settled down to a life of farming. He learned to drive a tractor, which brought him better pay and made his work easier, but he still dreamed of moving to Memphis and making his living by playing the music he loved.

One day, Riley accidentally crashed his boss's tractor. He was too ashamed and afraid to face his boss, so he decided to leave town. He didn't even wait to collect pay for a whole week of work. With only $2.50 in his pocket, he hitchhiked to Memphis. Later, he said that the first time he heard the musicians playing up and down Beale Street, he felt "like a kid in a candy store."

Beale Street

Beale Street was the main street in Memphis where all the African American blues and jazz musicians gathered to play. It was a paradise for a young musician like Riley. He stayed for a while in Memphis, soaking up as much music as he could. He learned a lot from watching and playing with other musicians.

Still, he didn't become famous. After a few uneventful months, he decided that playing on Beale Street wasn't the formula for success he had hoped it would be. He also missed his wife and felt guilty about leaving her—and about the damaged tractor. He returned to Indianola.

Riley paid the farmer back for the tractor repairs and returned to working on the plantation. He couldn't forget his dream of becoming a famous blues singer, though. He and his wife moved to Memphis the next year, ready to try again. This time, he would have better luck. His great talent would soon be recognized.

On the Air

At that time, most radio stations didn't play much African American music. One station, WDIA, decided to attract more listeners by playing blues and jazz. Riley B. King got a job at that station, singing and advertising a medicine called "Pepticon." He also got a job playing at a restaurant. People who heard him playing on the radio went to see him play live at the restaurant. He drew large audiences, and his musical career truly began to take off.

From Beale Street Blues Boy to B. B.

The people at the WDIA radio station wanted to give Riley B. King a new, catchier name. They called him Beale Street Blues Boy, because he got his start on Beale Street. That was a mouthful. After a while, they shortened it to Blues Boy King, but even that was too long. He became Bee Bee King and, finally, B. B. King. That name stuck.

B. B. had a great radio voice. Although he had a slight stutter, when he spoke on the radio, the stutter was hardly noticeable. He would slow down and speak simply and directly to his listeners. People liked his manner. They would write to him, asking him to play their favorite songs, and he became a popular disc jockey at the station.

Rising Fame

By 1950, B. B. King had his own radio show. He played a wide variety of music, but he never played recordings of his own music. He felt that playing his own music on his show would be like bragging.

One of B. B.'s favorite songs was "Three O'Clock Blues," by Lowell Fulson. B. B. King was one of the few disc jockeys playing it at that time. He played it over and over again. Fulson was moved by how much B. B. admired the song, so he agreed to let B. B. record a new version.

"Three O'Clock Blues" made B. B. King a national star. For five weeks in 1952, B. B. King's recording of the song was the best-selling blues record in the country. Suddenly, everyone wanted to hear B. B. King play. He started touring, traveling all around the country to play concerts.

B. B. King, 1948

B. B. King's growing career required a lot of work. He kept recording new hits and touring. As he became more successful, he hired other musicians to back him up and tour with him. He even bought a bus so that he and his band could travel more easily. He worked hard, playing concerts night after night in different towns. Out of the 366 days in the year 1956, there were only 24 nights when he didn't play!

Jazz and Blues in the 1940s and 1950s

B. B. King's music came from a rich blues and jazz background. Here are a few of the great artists whom B. B. King admired:

Blind Lemon Jefferson
Benny Goodman
Leadbelly
Lonnie Johnson

Charlie Christian
T-Bone Walker
Django Reinhardt
Muddy Waters

Benny Goodman

Django Reinhardt

B. B. King has said that his wife used to call him "Ol' Lemon Face" because of the way his face wrinkles up when he plays.

You Don't Have to Be Sad to Sing the Blues

When you listen to B. B. King playing and singing the blues, you can hear the depths of his emotions. In concerts, you can see his face wrinkle up and his eyes squeeze shut. Sometimes he wails the song at the top of his voice. Sometimes he moans the notes. But even when he is singing the most heartbreaking songs, you can hear a joyful love of music in his voice. He is totally passionate about playing the blues.

Lucille

When B. B. plays, he switches back and forth between singing and making his guitar sing. He thinks of his guitar as a woman with a beautiful voice. The guitar even has a name—Lucille. Lucille got her name one night when B. B. King ran out of a burning building. Suddenly, he realized that his guitar was still in the building. He ran back inside and grabbed his guitar, barely making it out alive. Later, he discovered that the fire had started when two men knocked over a kerosene heater. They had had a conflict about a woman named Lucille. After that, B. B. named all of his guitars Lucille so he would remember to take good care of them.

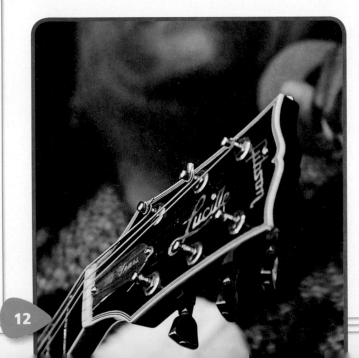

B. B. King often poses for photographs with Lucille.

More than once, B. B. had a guitar stolen from him. One time when this happened, he didn't have money for a new one. He needed a guitar to play his concerts. Although he knew it was wrong, he sneaked into a church and borrowed the pastor's guitar. After the concert, on his way back to the church to return the guitar, he was involved in a car accident. Amazingly, the guitar and everyone in the car escaped unharmed. B. B. returned the guitar and left some money inside it.

Reaching Everyone

In the 1960s, B. B. King's music was played in African American households throughout the country. Still, it bothered B. B. that his audience was mostly limited to African Americans. He wanted his music to reach *everyone*.

What B. B. King didn't realize at first was that there were already a lot of musicians, not only African Americans, who had been deeply influenced by his songs. Among these fans were British groups such as the Rolling Stones.

In 1969, B. B. King plays with rock 'n' roll musicians in New York City's Central Park.

These musicians were B. B. King's key to reaching a wider audience. One of them, Paul Butterfield, started a successful blues band. When people asked the band's lead guitarist, Mike Bloomfield, how he learned to play the blues, he replied, "by copying B. B.'s licks." When they asked, "B. B. who?" Bloomfield would say, "The real monster… B. B. King." This made the band's audiences want to find out more about this B. B. King, and when they did, they liked what they heard.

The destruction of the wall between blues singers and the wider musical audience came during this time of change. On February 26, 1967, B. B. King played at the Fillmore Auditorium in San Francisco to a crowd made up of all kinds of people. When he came on stage, they gave him a standing ovation that brought tears to his eyes. Then, in 1969, B. B. recorded a song that made him a national celebrity. It was called "The Thrill Is Gone."

A Likable Guy

People like B. B. King not only because of his music, but also because of his personality. In his autobiography, he wrote, "If I'm working with you and I sense you're feeling a little insecure, I try to make you feel great."

From the time he was young, he has had mature insights into people's emotional responses. Before his mother died, she told him to always be kind to people, and that people would love him if he showed them love. B. B. has always lived by these words. If someone was mean to him, his "revenge was to change a bad feeling into a good one." One person said about him that "if we had pictures instead of words in the dictionary, under the word 'gracious' would have to be B. B. King."

Little Kids Rock

When B. B. King was a child, music meant everything to him. To help other children add music to their lives, B. B. became a member of a program called Little Kids Rock. Little Kids Rock gives instruments and music instruction to schools without their own music programs.

Controlling Diabetes

Later in his life, B. B. King learned that he had diabetes. With this disease, your body has difficulty handling the sugar from the foods you eat. Your blood sugar levels don't stay stable, and this can cause serious health problems. Fortunately, diabetes can be controlled. B. B. did many things to manage his diabetes, such as watching his diet, leading a healthier lifestyle, and testing his blood sugar regularly.

Testing blood sugar usually involves pricking a finger to get a small blood sample. B. B. was afraid that if he pricked his fingers, he wouldn't be able to play his guitar as well. So he found a type of blood sugar test that he could use on his arm instead of on his fingers.

Honoring B. B. King

B. B. King is widely celebrated as the King of the Blues. There are many publications about him. Fans yearn to own autographed "Lucille edition" copies of his guitar. Here are just a few of the awards he has earned:

★ B. B. King was one of the first musicians inducted into the Rock and Roll Hall of Fame.

★ B. B. King has won more than a dozen Grammy Awards, including a special Grammy Lifetime Achievement Award.

★ In 2006, President George W. Bush awarded B. B. King the Presidential Medal of Freedom, the highest award given by the American government to a civilian.

Mississippi's Own

Mississippi is proud to be B. B. King's home state. Every year, Indianola holds a B. B. King Homecoming Festival. Indianola also has a museum dedicated to him, and several streets in the state are named after him and his guitar.

Long-Lasting Musical Influence

To most musicians, the sound of B. B. King's guitar is instantly recognizable. He has a style all his own. B. B. is also a role model when it comes to being a great performer. There are dozens of famous musicians who credit B. B. King with inspiring and influencing their careers.

After a concert, Elvis Presley was heard telling B. B. King, "Thanks, man, for the early lessons you gave me."

Eric Clapton has said about B. B. King, "I think he taps into something that is universal." He has also said that he doesn't think there is a better blues guitarist in the world than B. B. King.

Bonnie Raitt says about B. B. King's singing and playing, "I can't separate his soul as a guitar player from his soul as a singer, because they both got me at the same time...."

When John Lennon of the Beatles was once asked what he'd like to be able to do, he said, "play guitar like B. B. King."

Responding

✔ **TARGET SKILL** **Fact and Opinion** Think about the facts and opinions the author gives about B. B. King. Then copy the chart below. Add complete facts and more opinions from the biography to complete the chart.

Fact	Opinion
?	B. B. had a great radio voice.
	?

Write About It

Text to Self B. B. King loves to play and sing the blues. Think of an activity you enjoy. Write a few paragraphs that tell a story showing how much you enjoy the activity.

✔ **TARGET SKILL** **Fact and Opinion** Decide whether an idea can be proved or is a feeling or belief.

✔ **TARGET STRATEGY** **Analyze/Evaluate** Think carefully about the text and form an opinion about it.

GENRE **Biography** tells about events in a person's life, written by another person.